I AM WITH SOLUTION, I REPRESENT SOLUTION, I AM SOLUTION

I AM WITH SOLUTION, I REPRESENT SOLUTION, I AM SOLUTION

BERNARD HOLMES

I am with solution, I represent solution, I am solution

Published by Spines
ISBN: 979-8-89383-171-9

ABOUT THE AUTHOR

Bernard Lamant Holmes, known as B.L.J., comes from a well-known respectful household and has been trained to know how to deal with the outside world's temptations and many packages they come in; he is from Rochester, N.Y. He graduated from John Marshall School and discovered that one of his many gifts is writing.

He started pursuing his talent at the age of twenty, and ever since Jesus has been in his life, and his work is dedicated to Jesus, the man that has always been with him since birth. What Bernard wants from everyone is to make wise decisions in life and cut down a huge percentage of violent thinking which leads to the penitentiary or the cemetery

I need people of all ages to understand that Jesus is the solver of all problems and to be forgiven, you must come to him with a sincere heart and repent to be forgiven because it does not matter what you have done and how many times you have done it; it's never too late to say father please forgive me, He is so much in love with you and his mercy is everlasting.

1

WHAT GOES AROUND COMES AROUND

This young man was known as the ladies man.

And even though he dumped and played them, he knew that he could have them many times over and over again.

He especially loved the part when the girl eyes said: "How could you be with her and dump Me?"

With an evil smile on his face he just dismisses her without a conscience but what goes around comes around and when it does it hits you heavy.

But you know his type. He hears the message, but fails to listen saying: "Well it's not going to happen to me."

So, one day he came home and found his mother crying.
Before he could say anything she said over and over again: "What he said, and what he promised, the whole time he was lying."

For a moment he felt like hitting the ceiling.

But he suddenly stopped and started thinking , and he realized that what his mom was feeling what the girls that he had mistreated in the past were feeling.

Letter to God

To the one man that shed's light in my dark tunnel, the man that repeatedly delivered me from the belly of the beast, the man that his mercy to me, as well as everybody else, is everlasting, the one who have been walking with me through the good times as well as the bad.

And it's no other than Jesus Christ, from the beginning to the end, the omega, the reason that I am here, the reason why I am writing these stories, the reason why he is working through me to save souls to deliver them from the belly of the beast as Jesus has done for me and to repay him is to help spread the word.

2

THE TRUE UNDERSTANDING OF LOVE

They say love does not live here anymore.

So what's all the hunting for a soul mate and dating for?

Because of love they say they have been used, under-appreciated and their self-esteem left

low.

They say why be the only odd one looking for someone no one is looking for so I just go with the flow.

They say their heart hurts so bad that it's to a point that it's unable to heal.

All love has done for me was leave me disappointed, broken and at the end, it couldn't care less how I feel.

The more I give to love the more love just takes and takes.

It seems like every time I think I found the one, they always turn out being a complete fake.

And after meeting Mr. or Ms. wrong for so long my mind got me asking what's next?

That's why sometimes they make me hate the opposite sex.

You see first things first when it comes to looking for a women or a man, you need to know what love requires and how to go about it or you will go through life and never understand.

So when I explain it to you, you will know this as well as the others.

True love has no requirements of weight, height or color.

True love has to make love to your mind before they make love in the bedroom.

True love, if they respect you they would respect the tradition by putting the honeymoon after the bride and the groom.

Now that's true love.

3

TV RAISED AND KILLED TIM

There were kids that learned everything on TV because their parents were too busy to teach them, so the TV taught them.

When they need information about anything the TV is what they turned to, so basically television raised them.

So the tragic ending of this story is the parents, for lack of focusing their attention on their

Kids.

After all of the books and television shows on how to be a good parent, you think some people would listen, but sometimes that's the way it is.

One day the kids was watching a Houdini show with the hocus pocus and make'em disappear before your very eyes.

But what the magician is doing is acting. None of it is real and that's what the kids do not understand or realize.

So they went to the pool unsupervised and performed the same trick that they saw on TV.

So Tim put on his swimming trunks and his sister Meloney wrapped the chains around him.

Now he went to the deep end to perform the unlock the lock and take off the chains trick and swim up to the top.

He wiggles, he's picking the lock and now he's not moving, after that Meloney noticed all the movement her brother made had suddenly stopped.

So she ran into the house to get their parents, and when they came out to get him out of the water, they performed CPR on him.

When they did not get a response, that's when the ambulance came to work on the kid. But the paramedics tried everything to save the child but they were unable to revive him.

4

TWO CHOICES ONLY ONE DECISION

Will you chose the light over the darkness?

Will you chose the kindhearted over the heartless?

Will you help the kids grow up with the things that will help them succeed?

Will you chose to follow the bad or unite with the good and help lead?

Will you take part in Jesus's plan for revolution, or will you chose to burn with the of the pollution?

Will you join us on our journey of finding some positive and religious thinkers for our children? Or will you be one of those people that will help to put suffering in the world and have positive things come to an end?

What I am saying is that there is a lot of choices, but the problem is which one is the right road to take.

One is a bright future, and the other one is you choose will be the biggest mistake you will ever make.

5

THE WORST DATING EXPERIENCE

There was a young lady that was desperate to get a man.

So she went to places like clubs, bars and even restaurants to look for a man.

She would at times daydream about being in a big wedding and walking down the aisle to be some lucky man's wife.

But when she snaps out of daydreaming she goes back to I can't find a man to save my

Life.

So one day she heard people at her job talking about internet dating.

As she continues to listen to her employees' conversation she heard them mention the hook up, creating your profile and mating.

Now after hearing that, she couldn't wait to get home, get on the internet, create her profile and wait for responses from men.

After thirty minutes she heard the computer say "you got mail" so she clicked on it and it showed ten.

So she went through the profile and picked the tenth guy and invited him over to her place Friday night.

When Friday night got here, she did detailed cleaning making sure everything was right.

So when he came over, she opened the door and said, "What's up?"

He said "Your hands." she said "huh my hands?" He said " Yea put'em up."

After tying her up he loads up the goodies and she says. "I thought you were a nice guy and now you do this to me?"

He said "First of all, you only know what I told you and you invited the same man into your home the next day and you don't even know me. So who is the fool you or me?"

6

NO MORE

NO MORE FILLING PEOPLE'S HEAD WITH ILLUSION.

No more prostitution.
No more babies being born deformed because of drugs.
No more people getting killed and infected by insects and bugs.
No more selling clothes with bad messages.
No more selling kids alcohol beverages.
No more covering the truth with a lie.
No more people refusing to try.
No More.

Keep your Reputation Positive

There was a young lady that slept around with almost everyone in her neighborhood and did not care who knew.

And for the men that like them type of women well I can't tell you what an enormous crowd it drew.

The part where she slept with a lot of men was bad but now knowing at least one of the men's name.

That's the part right there that drew shame.

A couple of people already told her if she continues to sleep around when you're ready to settle down no man will deal with you.

But you know what females like her response is? " Well I'm grown and I am going to do what I want to do."

So years pass by and she decides to slow down and be in a one- on-one relationship and talk to men that she likes.

But the thing is not one of the men that she tried to talk to would bite.

And the reason why is because they knew about her.

Meaning in the past they knew what kind of person she were.

Now after being avoided by every man that she tried to talk to she goes back to her table with a sad look on her face and a drink in her hand.

Then a young man came over to see why she was so sad and after she told him he said "When your reputation is ruined like that, it's impossible to have friends or a man."

How Many

How many people shout out the lords name?

And how many people go to church so the preacher can shake their hand saying I'm glad you came?

How many people you see showing up for an interview?

Or building up what they took down by not only starting fresh but new?

How many people out there help these kids when it comes to knowledge?

Especially the type that will get them into college?

How many people you see helping us fight for what's right?

Saying man I finally see the light.

How many people you hear say man I need to break this chain?

And stop causing my people pain.

Not many.

It Takes One to Know One

An elder and a young man was having a conversation about change.

And the youngster said the things that he had done it is too late to start fresh and he cannot change the past and nether can it be rearranged.

He said he had done so much bad in his life that he felt that if he started it he should finish it.

And the elder said to him that "Even though you have done wrong all of your life it's never too late to get on the right track and you are still in it to win it. "

The youngster said, "Hey I'm going to go out the way I'm going to go out."

The elder said, "Let me tell you a story on how the choice I'm trying to give you gave this person in this story a way out."

He said, "There was a young man about your age he grew up around bad influences and areas where if the wrong person from the wrong side of town came through they will burry ya."

"He went from selling drugs to being in gangs and of those activities caused him incarceration time."

"He was in and out of jail mostly in for crimes of all kinds."

The young man said, "Not to cut you off, but you have to go through what I have been through to be my teacher."

The elder said, "Who do you think this story is about? Because the man before you hasn't always been a preacher."

Learn Now, be Tested Later vol. 1

One day this father took his two kids to the playground and the kids thought they were going to play. Well they were wrong.

The minute their father had them sit on the bench, the kids knew it was going to be the type of talk that is boring and long.

So the father asked his son a question about what would you do if you woke up and there was a fire in the house.

Both kids were so shocked to be asked that question they just sat there quiet as a mouse.

The father said, " Go ahead and give it a try you might answer right but until you try you will never know."

So both kids said, "Dad we honestly don't know."

Then what he did was tell them what and how to do things , step by step, and he also gave them a paper with directions on it for them to keep.

And after he told them what to do he said, "Make sure you memorize these steps because failing to do so the consequences can be pretty steep."

One night a fire broke out and the kids woke up and smelled smoke so they got up and open the bedroom door and they saw the fire spreading everywhere.

After seeing that the kids remembered what their father said and followed the steps and last but not least they opened their bedroom window and got out of there.

When the fire department arrived there everyone had been already been out of the house and taken to the hospital just to make sure the family was ok before their release.

And the parents was so proud of them for listening, following directions and remembering what to do they decided to reward them by taking them to Chucky Cheese.

If it wasn't for them

If it wasn't for them we would be still sitting in the back of the bus.

If it wasn't for them we would not have them recipes, culture, hope and prayer that they have taught us.

If it wasn't for them Barack Obama wouldn't be allowed to be in the league period to get elected.

If it wasn't for them our rights to do anything would have never been started or protected.

If it wasn't for them we would have looked at our skin color like a prison.

If it wasn't for them we would have never overcome our mission.

If it wasn't for them, there's an old saying, "They can throw us in jail, they can take our life but they can take what we have up here."

That's why like technology our mind is advancing in this world quickly and everywhere.

Guns

If you do not think guns are trouble then ask some of the people in prison for 15 years to life and I know they wish they had made a better decision.

The percentage of people carrying illegal guns is more than average.

And that's crazy because there are more people with guns than people with badges.

Some use it for protection and others use it for other reasons.

Rather it's robbing or shooting an intruder for treason.

So when you're thinking about guns ask yourself these questions.

Like will this gun bring out the worse of me or will I learn a hard or easy lesson.

Grown and Dead

This young lady felt that just because she is 18 that she knew everything and could come in her parent's house all hours of the night.

And there were many times when her parent's told her about the streets but to her she felt that what her parents were saying was wrong and what she was doing was right.

So her parent's said this, "You may be grown and if you want to see another birthday, then we suggest at night you stay home."

"Because when your'e out there we worry and we are afraid of getting that call and your mother and I end up breaking down over the phone."

With that being said she chose to ignore her parent's warning and continue to roam the streets and come home whenever she wanted to.

So a week later, they knew something was wrong because she was never gone for this long so they called the cops to report the daughter missing so the cops can do what they do.

Three hours later the police had discovered a body in the alley so they took it over to the morgue and also taking the parents over to identify the body if they were able.

As the morgue doctor pulls back the sheet enough for them to see and they burst into tears as they saw there daughter laying on the table

Drugs, Murder and Regrets

I'm going to tell you a story

When I am through telling you this story I really hope that this lesson helps more than just me.

I am going to tell you the reason why I am the cost of my little brother's death.

It involves me, my stupidity, thinking, and drugs like weed, cocaine and crystal meth.

I had a shoe box that I put up high enough. To make sure my little brother did not go into the box I wrote on the front "Do not touch."

So when I left to go to work, my brother came in through the back door.

When he went into our bedroom, he must have spotted the shoe box that I put on the shelf wondering what I used it for.

He grabbed a chair from the desk and took the box.

Now when he opened it he probably thought it was candy that was shaped like small rocks.

As soon as he tasted one he quickly had a strong addiction.

When he was done trying all of the drugs he noticed his body in a painful and critical condition.

He fell to the floor and started shaking.

My mother walks in fifteen minutes later finding her son on the ground laying lifeless, she screamed out, "Nathen!"

She quickly ran to call 911 and told them the situation.

When the paramedics came to check him out, they tried everything to revive him but they told her that he was gone. Now it's been 20 years since my mother and I had contact or had a decent conversation.

Good Person, Bad Company= Horrible Future

This young man had a friend that peer-pressured him into doing dangerous things to earn strips or better yet earn street credit.

And he always told him not to worry about getting into trouble because I will always keep you well protected.

The thing that he liked about his friend is that he did not have a mind of his own.

He also knew that he was as bright as a bag of stones.

So to convince him, he told him that he had been doing this for years and he had not been caught yet.

"And furthermore, the job that you have, you are behind on bills so I am giving you this opportunity to clear out your debt."

He thought about what his friend said about the bills and went with his friend to help break in a house the next street over to steal whatever had value to them and went back to his house to spilt what they had stolen.

So his friend says to him, " See, piece of cake," and that's when he started believing his troublemaking friend and decided to continue on breaking into houses for and for a while they were rollin.

But one day, they saw this family bringing in a lot of merchandise that kept them staring at them as they brought them in the house.

The next day the two boys did a stake- out and when the time is right they would make there move after everyone had bounced.

After seeing everyone leave, they went right to work and came in through the back door.

As soon as they got in they saw that 60 inch TV and their eyes couldn't help but to glow.

The minute they put their foot to go into the living room the security system alarm went off loud enough for the neighbors to hear.

When the young men made a break for it, and escaped out the way they came, the police had all escape routes shut down everywhere.

When they came before the judge he gave them a prison sentence of 5,475 days.

Now they have to spend 15 years of their lives in a dreadful place but it's like the old saying goes, if you want to see your future tomorrow look at your friends today.

Drugs and their Causes

When drugs have been injected inter your system it messes up your entire body rhythm.

And certain types of drugs attack your heart. It will tear your entire body apart.

Does it matter what type of drugs it's a yes and a no but the thing is it's only a matter of time

Some can't do too much harm to you and there are others that can put your life on the line,

And that alone is a serious sign.

Plus, it can change your looks, self-esteem and your hygiene.

It will also turn you into a person you or the people you know have never seen.

So the next time when you are thinking about taking drugs to solve your problems

You just turn your head away and hold your head up high and say I am better without them.

Because of Them

Because of them they invented the open heart surgery.

Because of them the states is designed perfectly.

Because of them every building is up today.

Because of them their their remembrance and inventions are celebrated every holiday.

Because of them our opportunities came in varieties in due time.

Because of them there is no more whites only and no coloreds allowed signs.

Because of them this whole world is ours and do not ever forget that.

And if it was not for them this world would not be on the level where it's at and that's a fact.

Anger

Anger, the real reason why a lot of decisions people make are in regret, the reason why people take other people's lives and the reason why a lot of people are in prison.

The reason why the decisions that people make turn into a natural disaster is because when people are in angry mode, the negative thoughts quickly come up rushing in and overflood the brain and kicks out the positive thoughts immediately which is the voice of reason. And even if anyone were to try to talk some sense into the person that is angry there is no room in that person's mind to listen.

And at that very moment when anger causes the person to make a bad decision that person ends up in a lot of trouble by other people or end up in prison due to the fact that anger would not allow them to control their actions and when they end up in regretful situations that's when the anger that they had in them is gone and now the voice of reason kicks in.

And when you get to that point where you are in a position living, eating, sleeping and socializing around people that have done just as bad or worse in the state pin.

Because of my Parents

If it was not for my parents I would be talking to them through plate glass.

I would not even have my career if I did not pass from class to class,

And if my home work was not done.

I could not go to the basket ball court to make any shot's and I mean not one.

I remember as a kid when my father ask me questions like what would I do in case of a

Fire.

My mother, she told me to always tell the truth because you make it bad for yourself when you are a liar.

But before they leave this earth they can say that they have raised a good young man.

A man that has for people of all ages a unique plan.

Black History

Black History was two weeks away and the teacher wanted the students to pick a person and do a report on them.

While everyone is working on their projects one student did not so the teacher asked why she is not doing her project like the rest of them.

The young lady said why should I honor certain people that is not here anymore.

Now I already know who they are and what they stood for.

Like the Nobel peace prize, the stuff they invented, fighting for our freedom and it hasen't gotten us anywhere.

The teacher said before you disrespect any further you need to keep your lips together and open your ears and put a q tip in one end so it will not go in one ear and out the other while you are still sitting here.

If it was not for them your choices would have been tricked.

And the way you think would have been fixed.

What that means is you still think the way they want you to think and feel about

Yourself.

For instance looking at your color as a prison and making you hate yourself and love their wealth.

If it was not for them the slave owner would have sold you for what you think you are

Worth.

Now after saying that I see a different expression on your face and I know the truth hurts.

As a matter of fact you should do your report on Madame Walker because if it was not for her, your hair would not be done by the salon every week.

Now I know I expect everyone's project in two weeks but I expect your project in one week.

Be Strong and Move On

When your loved one says it's over, please accept it and move on.

I mean what are you going to do be a lop sided lover for this person when there's plenty of fish in the sea I mean come on.

Yea we miss the times that we spend with them, and the things that we used to do, but understand this it's all in the past.

Because when you let people including the person you want to be with, doing that, they know that your'e weak, pathetic, and you have no game and no class.

And do not do things like stalking or trying to interfere with that person's relationship because it will not get that person back. You will only make it worse.

Now for the ones that do not know, you need to understand this before you continue to make a fool out of yourself you cannot make someone want you by force.

Remember, you would want to love someone the same exact way you would want to be loved in return.

Or will you kill or be killed over someone that does not want you anymore so pick the smart way instead of the hard way to learn.

· · ·

A Simple Weapon Cost his Freedom

This young man that brought a gun because being protected and safe is how he should always feel.

But little do he know that a lot of people that have been in trouble in many ways behind a piece of steel.

Now after purchasing the gun he couldn't feel even better having protection at his side at all time.

When it comes to working at any shift it was no longer a problem. He would work all hours at any shift and at anytime.

So one day, he headed out the door for work when he bumped into his misery loves company baby mother.

And she get's in his face telling him how he's not doing enough to support their son as she continues with the insults one after another.

But what sent him over the edge is when she threaten to not let him see his kid.

So when he heard that, she never seen someone so violent and so much in a rage when he flipped the lid.

So that's when he pulled out his gun and said "If my kid cannot see me the he defiantly will not see you."

As he shoots and kills her he runs when he hears sirens and soon finds himself surrounded and his only option was to give up, What else could he do?

Now he is given the sentence of 20 years in prison behind a simple piece of steel.

Where he will be on a 23 hour lockdown and everyday being served 3 unfit meals.

. . .

A Message on Jokes

Jokes, they're funny, they keep you happy, liking the response of laughter and it's useful when your'e killing time.

But there is another group or audience that find it offensive and that's when you have crossed the line.

Because of people's so call harmless jokes other people have been hurt, sad, crying, fighting and even committed suicide because of it.

And then the one that is making the jokes should look at themselves because they are not what you call picture perfect.

Now when someone talks about another person they are really talking about themselves. They just have your name mixed up in it.

When people do teasing, years down the line, they will forget. But the ones that have been teased will never forget it.

So next time you have a joke about someone, please keep it to yourself because whether you know it or not, you can do them damage permanently.

And always remember whatever you say or do make sure you keep the RESPECT.

A Real Christmas Gift

There was a young man who thought that the meaning of Christmas was to receive expensive and big gifts to unwrap on Christmas day.

So while he is receiving gifts every year from family and friends, he fails to realize and appreciate the true gifts somewhere along the way.

Now every Christmas he had was great, exciting and expensive except for this Christmas where he received nothing.

So he got upset and decided to get out of the house for a while and mumbling how could they just not get me anything, it don't have to be much but at least give something.

Then he walked around until he came across a homeless person that was filled with so much joy it was like he was smiling like there was no tomorrow.

So he just stood there looking at him being filled with the opposite of sorrow.

Then the homeless person asked the young man what's with the long face on Christmas day.

Then the young man told the homeless man how he saw presents around the tree and not one had his name on it, "So yea to me it is not Christmas day."

Now after listening to the young man the homeless man said to him, "Son I will give you a present but this present does not come with wrapping paper or a bow."

And he said this to him, "Give and it will be given in good measure. For whatever measure you deal out to others it will be dealt to you in return."

That is something for the rest of your days that shall always be taught and learned.

A Players Last Play

There was a young man that liked to sleep with women whether they have a boyfriend or are married.

And people warned him that doing what he is doing will lead to two outcomes you looking over your shoulders, or loved ones picking the place where they want you buried.

But in his mind he felt that as long as he stayed sneaky,

And the women that he went to bed with remain easy,

He figured "how could he go wrong?"

But what he does not realize is that being slick and slide can only last for so long.

One day he met this woman that was married and she made an arrangement for him to come to the house when her husband was at work.

When the neighbor saw what was going on, he thought not telling put's guilt on him but he knew that the truth shall set him free even though the married man would be hurt.

So when the neighbor told the married man that some guy was sleeping with his wife a lot of foul and evil thought's quickly fills up his head.

Later on that night neighbors said that voices were shouting in a jealous rage saying something about who did you have in my bed.

By the next day the married women and the player that like to sleep with women whether they are married or not was found in the dumpster dead.

A Message in Respect

Yes when we see women we lust, fantasize and hormones rages out of control.

But before you make the biggest mistake of your life by messing with someone who is with somebody that's when you need to slow your roll.

See the thing is when you just do and don't think about the consequences at the moment it just feels right to you.

But when later comes that's when you worry because that person is looking for you.

Millions of people get hurt or killed behind messing with someone that has somebody.

And sadly the numbers continue to grow highly.

Now if you don't believe me then have a talk with some of the people in the penitentiary.

Or better yet have a chat with the people that learned their lesson in a tragic way in the cemetery.

A Message on Sex

To whoever told you that, "It's not a big deal, Its just sex" they're negligent.

Because believing them will have you at the clinic or on a new episode of sixteen and

Pregnant.

So when your boyfriend or girlfriend tells you that sex is only a three letter word.

Please at all costs, kick him or her and what they said to the curve.

Because when the weak moment happens there's no turning back the hands of time or singing your should've, could've , would've, it's been done.

Understand this there's certain things you get a second chance on but when it comes to your life, you only get one.

And just because they look good and look clean.

It does not mean that they are clean and understand this things are not what they seem.

So next time when your boyfriend or girlfriend wants you to put out make sure you stay alert, keep your guards up and be aware.

Because if you do not care then they will not care.

A loved One's Prayer

It's a sad day when our love one goes to the light.

Even though it's been said it's not fair but it's right.

But we appreciate the time that we spent with them while they was here.

When we was at our weakest they was right there.

We will always miss them forever, forget them never.

Because to forget them is to forget the skills that they taught us everyday that makes us better and better.

And as long as we are here their memory will always be here.

Through our eyes our love ones will continue to live and see the world through our eyes.

And it has been said lord when it is our turn to see you we must come prepared or not prepared.

Lord we thank you for blessing one of your children into your kingdom where there is no more violence, no more pain and no more tears.

And I will be waiting on the day for us to meet again.

In the name of your son Jesus Christ our lord and personal savior we pray amen.

A kids Quest for Peace

There was a young man that lived each day in terror.

Because being teased so bad threw his self-esteem from a hundred percent to a zero minus, He was even ashamed to look at his reflection in the mirror.

I mean everyday from and to school being teased, being looked at as a freak I mean how much can he take?

For a minute he thought that teasing was only temporary or maybe it's just fate.

Because of their comments towards him sometimes he can hold back his tears and most of the time he sat there and cried.

Thinking how could he stop this from continuing to happen, should he run away or should he end this pain and commit suicide.

So before he committed suicide he wrote a note that said, "lord when I see you please give me what I lack to get on this earth like good friends, peace and respect."

"Because the last thing I need is to be looked at as a freak and a outcast and once again being just another reject."

"I cannot take another second going through the humiliation of being horribly teased over and over again."

"And all I ask for is when I see you in heaven is that I receive the opposite of what I have been getting from earth and in Jesus name amen."

. . .

A message in hard work

Every since I was old enough to work,

Everyday I have been asking myself What's the worth?

And my body as well as my pockets be the only one that hurts.

Taking orders after orders ,being cursed out by the boss,

Working crazy hours while my summer passes by and I'm thinking to myself what a terrible loss.

After earning all of that money that I have made,

I hardly had enough time to enjoy myself sitting at the beach and using a huge umbrella for shade.

The days that I get off it is always too short and never enough time to enjoy them.

It makes you wonder why you cannot hit the lotto like the rest of them.

Sometimes I wonder how I go from I have a day off or two yessss, yahoo, amen.

To aww man that went by too quick now it's back to work again.

But after all that complaining I'm glad I was here.

Because believe or not, not many people can get a job anywhere.

7

THE BULLY VS HIS MATCH VOL. 1

There was a bully in school that everyone was afraid of.

The bully is the type of person that constantly terrorizes you until he decides when enough is enough.

So when class started, the bully spotted this student that came in late so he began picking on the student because he was overweight.

And the bully continued to make the student feel bad by talking about how big the student is and how much he ate.

On the way home the student felt bad about being teased and decided to do something about it.

So he goes to his parent's room and got the gun from the closet and said "This is how I am going to go about it."

The next day he went to his classes but the last class was the one that the bully was in.

As soon as he stepped into the class, the bully spotted him and that's when the teasing began.

The bully did things like shoving, hitting and tripping him and the student's anger get pushed to the limit.

The bully continued with the mental as well as the physical insults telling him "You know you are afraid of me admit it."

So the student stood up and said, "Yea I'm afraid, but I know what you are afraid of."

The bully said, "Afraid of what?" The student said this and pulled out the gun and shot the bully to death leaving the student covered in the bully's blood.

8

SURVIVING YOUR PARENT'S BREAK- UP

Sometimes it feels like your world is ending when your parent's say their relationship is not working.

And you will be the one hurting.

Now the memories like your mom and dad relaxing in the shade and sipping on lemonade, just seeing you and your family having a picnic in the park.

But the memories that you have of yore will never be forgotten because it will always be in your heart.

Who knows maybe they will get back together again or they might stay separated.

Seeing one parent at certain times can get complicated.

For a youngster It's hard to keep your head up.

Because on the inside you feel all torn up.

Just remember that the house has changed.

But their love for you will always remain the same.

9

———

RESPONSIBILITY AND PREPARING

This young lady's parents called her to the table to talk to her about responsibilities and preparing.

While they were telling her what they were doing and why, the young lady looked at her parents as if she couldn't believe what she was hearing.

So the parents continued with the conversation telling her to get her started to pay bills we only want you to give us twenty five dollars a week.

Their daughter says twenty five dollars a week to me that's a little steep.

The parents said you get $400 a week and you cannot give $25.00 a week for rent?

The daughter said, "Well I know about the world and I know what to do so why should I give you guys one red cent."

Then she went to get her own place thinking that she had the whole world figured out.

Well, not long after she got her place that she was not ready for, because bills were piling up everywhere and she was one notice away from being kicked out.

So she called the home of the parents for their advice that she took for granted.

The parents answer the phone and say "Is this the same daughter that she was at the top and on her butt she very soon landed?"

"Remember when we tried to get you prepared for the world and you told us that we can take our getting ready for the world system and shove it?"

And now you come back to us because you were not ready and I know you don't want to hear this but saying I told you so just does not quite put it.

10

RESPECT YOUR MIRROR IMAGE

There was a young man that did not have or show respect for his elders or should I say, the ones who paved the way for the upcoming generation.

Now, instead of him looking at the elders as a waste of life, he should be looking to them as an inspiration.

So one day one of the elders said to him "Young man no matter what you say or think about us always remember this: you are what you mock."

And they told him, "It may not mean nothing now but later on in life it will mean a lot."

So after hearing those words of wisdom, it travels to this young man like the rest of the information travels through a lot of people's minds, going in one ear and out the other.

And it happens from generation to generation and one after another.

Now, when later on came he got the rankled skin, the cane and taking him five minutes to walk across the street, and constantly needs help bathing, eating and putting on his socks and shoes on his feet.

So one day he was walking across the street and the young man in the car was impatiently waiting for the old man to cross the street.

And of course the comment the young man in the car made was cold.

So the comment he made was said like this, "How many days does it take you to cross the street, It's not my fault your old."

That comment alone reminded him of how he treated the older people when he was that young man's age.

But the funny thing was he did not feel any kind of rage.

Why? Because he remembered what the elder said to him growing up and it was often said to him a lot.

No matter what you say or think about us always remember this you are what you mock.

11

RESPECT THE RING

The ring that you see on the spouse's finger is to be respected.

Because if it's not, then there is no bodyguard that can keep you well protected.

When you mess with someone's spouse, the first reaction is anger.

Then the next reaction is your body is in serious danger.

Some say it's ok to fantasize about a married spouse.

Thinking about the sexy wear they would be in for you while romance takes place all over the house.

But here's the problem acting on it is just a baby step away from taking place.

The main clues is the two of you alone, a strong drink and love showing all over your face.

And the biggest mistake of your life happens when the two of you end up sleeping together.

Now when that happens and the spouse finds out you could be looking over your shoulders forever.

12

PARENT'S BEFORE THEIR TIME

For those that say raising kids is easy,

I got news for you from what I have seen it's almost impossible believe me.

Before you get caught up in the web I better scare you away and have you come to your senses.

And tell you about the baby expenses.

You have things like clothing, pacifier, baby food, car seat, walker, play pen and diapers.

Now for people that are full grown they are still not ready and if they are not ready then do you think it's going to be for you as a minor?

If you want to take care of something get a pet and look at it as a baby.

Because bringing babies in this world does not determine rather you are a man or a Woman.

13

ONE DEAD, ONE IN PRISON, STILL
AVAILABLE

Two men are fighting over a women that is not even worth fighting for.

Their words, expression and voice alone was past hardcore.

Their argument drew an enormous crowd.

As they exchange words to each other out loud.

The deeper the argument got,

The closer they came to fighting or one of them getting shot.

So one of the two gentlemen decided to settle the argument with the solution.

Then without hesitation one of them pulled out a gun and shot the other and now he's heading back to the house on the run.

Now one is dead,

And the other one was picked up the same day by the feds.

Why instead of handling the situation positively and professionally

They decided to act like complete animals.

At the end no one wins one is dead and the other is in prison so who gets the girl? Neither one is available.

And at the end after all of the arguing, fighting and bloodshed the women is still available.

14

LETTER TO GOD

To the one man that shed's light in my dark tunnel, the man that repeatedly delivered me from the belly of the beast, the man that his mercy to me, as well as everybody else, is everlasting, the one who have been walking with me through the good times as well as the bad.

And it's no other than Jesus Christ, from the beginning to the end, the omega, the reason that I am here, the reason why I am writing these stories, the reason why he is working through me to save souls to deliver them from the belly of the beast as Jesus has done for me and to repay him is to help spread the word.